Zoey meets David

Pat Tolve

Archway Publishing
1663 Liberty Drive
Bloomington, IN 47403
www.archwaypublishing.com
844-669-3957

ISBN: 978-1-6657-0358-1 (sc)
ISBN: 978-1-6657-0359-8 (hc)
ISBN: 978-1-6657-0360-4 (e)

Archway Publishing rev. date: 05/10/2021

To my husband, Dave, for always being there for me. And my children, Tommy, David and Michael, you can do whatever you set your minds to.

One day my mom and I went for pizza. As we walked in, on the wall was an advertisement about puppies for sale. Chinese Crested puppies. My mom was excited. You see, she always wanted one.

So, as I was sitting and waiting for my pizza my mom went to the wall where the advertisement was. It read: Chinese Crested puppies for sale. My mom was excited. As I was eating my pizza, my mom made a phone call. "Do you have any hairless puppies left?" my mom asked. "No," the woman stated. "But I have a few Powder Puffs left." "Where are you?" asked my mom. "I have a pet grooming place on Halstead Avenue," she replied. "Oh, my goodness!" my mom shouted, "I am right down the street, I will be right there."

We hurried to finish our pizza and rushed to the car so we can go see the puppies. As we were climbing the stairs to the store, a woman passed us. We opened the door and walked in. In the middle of the room, to my moms' surprise, there she was. The most beautiful puppy I have ever seen. "I thought you didn't have any hairless puppies?" said mom. The store owner looked upset. "The lady who just left returned her," she stated! "I am shocked!" "She was her second owner! I can't believe she returned her," she continued "She told me that she cried all day and night."

The puppy was running around with her brothers and sisters as David watched them. "David, sit down on the floor to see if she comes to you." My mom said. My mom was so excited. The puppy ran up to me and sat in my lap. She was sitting just looking at me.

"We will take her." my mom said. The woman explained to us that we would be her third owner. "Puppies need a lot of attention," the store owner said. My mom assured her and told the woman that we would take incredibly good care of her and promised her that we will be her last owner. My mom always wanted to rescue a dog. My mom paid the store owner and picked up the puppy. We then called my dad. My dad came to the store and was shocked. You see she had no fur on her body other than the long mane down her back, and some hair on her tail, head and paws. She was beautiful, yet different. "Do you really want that?" he asked. "Don't you want a dog with fur?" "No" my mom said, "She is perfect."

We bought everything a new puppy would want. Toys, food and a bed to welcome her to her new home. When we got home, my mom asked, "What do you want to name her?" "Zoey," I said. "Then Zoey it is," said my mom. The first thing I did was walked her around our backyard and watched her smell and jump around. "Zoey" David called, just then Zoey turned around and looked at David. "He will be my family," she said. "I will love him with everything in me for all my life".

The yard was big. Zoey ran and jumped around and then walked to the next yard. "Zoey!" screamed David. But she just kept walking. David screamed her name and started to cry. His mom came outside to see what was happening. And a neighbor opened her window to ask what was wrong. "Zoey is walking away from me," cried David.

Then Zoey stopped and turned around. "I upset my David," she thought. Zoey ran up to him and licked his tears off his face. Zoey said to herself "I just wanted to explore; I did not mean to make you cry". My mom ran over to us. "David," she said. "Zoey is a baby, a puppy. She needs a leash on her for her safety". My mom attached the leash and then Zoey followed David, back to the house.

Zoey spent the next hour playing in the yard with David. "I will never again walk away from him," Zoey said to herself. She had so much fun with David. She Jumped all around and explored her new home. His mom came outside and talked to us. She was telling David that he needed to be responsible for me. He would be the one feeding and walking me outside.

David showed Zoey all the colorful fish swimming in the pond. They played ball and chased each other around the yard. They played until the sun went down. "I am exhausted, David and I had so much fun and it was only our first day together." Zoey thought.

David and Zoey went inside after a long day of fun. They were both tired after all the playing. David put down Zoey's water and food. David stood and watched her eat. He had the biggest smile on his face. "I think I will like it here," said Zoey.

Then David moved Zoey's bed into his room. It was time to sleep. "Good Night Zoey," David whispered. Zoey just looked up at him and stared. "Our adventure has just started," she thought to herself. "and David, does not even know it. David does not know that he will be the most important human in my life. It took three families to find my forever home. David makes me feel so good. He makes me feel special, wanted, and most importantly loved. I guess three times is a charm." Zoey thought

Pat Tolve lives in Harrison, New York. She stayed home to raise her three children. Two of those children were born premature and one of those children has special needs. She has always had a soft heart for animals that need a home especially those with special needs. Since the adoption of Zoey, Tolve has rescued two other dogs, all with special needs.

Printed in the United States
by Baker & Taylor Publisher Services